ENVIRONMENTAL HEALTH IN SELECTED ASIAN COUNTRIES

ISBN 978 92 9061 838 6

Suggested citation. Environmental health in selected Asian countries. Manila, Philippines. World Health Organization Regional Office for the Western Pacific; 2018. Licence: CC BY-NC-SA 3.0 IGO.

Cataloguing-in-Publication (CIP) data. 1. Asia. 2. Environmental health. I. World Health Organization Regional Office for the Western Pacific. (NLM Classification: WA30.5).

CONTENTS

Foreword	iv
Acknowledgements	vi
Abbreviations	vii
Introduction	1
The burden of disease from environmental risks	5
Environment and health in the context of the SDGs	9
End hunger, achieve food security and improved nutrition and promote sustainable agriculture (SDG 2)	11
Ensure availability and sustainable management of water and sanitation for all (SDG 6)	17
Ensure access to affordable, reliable, sustainable and modern energy for all (SDG 7)	23
Make cities and human settlements inclusive, safe, resilient and sustainable (SDG 11)	27
Take urgent action to combat climate change and its impacts (SDG 13)	33
Ensure healthy lives and promote well-being for all at all ages (SDG 3)	39
Emerging challenges	47
Conclusions	51
References	52

FOREWORD

This report was prepared for the Asia-Pacific Regional Forum on Health and Environment held on 6–8 October 2016 in Manila, Philippines. The report presents the state of the environment and health in the 14 countries of the Regional Forum, based on country profiles and United Nations and World Health Organization statistics. This updated version incorporates inputs from Member States at the Regional Forum.

The report provides a snapshot of progress among these countries on relevant Sustainable Development Goals (SDGs): SDG 2 (End hunger, achieve food security and improved nutrition and promote sustainable agriculture); SDG 3 (Ensure healthy lives and promote well-being for all at all ages); SDG 6 (Ensure availability and sustainable management of water and sanitation for all); SDG 7 (Ensure access to affordable, reliable, sustainable and modern energy for all); SDG 11 (Make cities and human settlements inclusive, safe, resilient and sustainable); and SDG 13 (Take urgent action to combat climate change and its impacts).

All countries are making advances in key areas of human development and health. Nevertheless, the impact of environmental risks on health is large. Of the 12.6 million deaths attributable globally to modifiable environmental risks, more than 4 million occurred in the 14 Forum countries, according to data from 2012. Most of these deaths (3.35 million) were from noncommunicable diseases, with air pollution playing a significant role.

There are significant differences among Regional Forum countries. For example, the age-standardized death rate from modifiable environmental risks varies among countries from around 40 to more than 300 per 100 000. Likewise, healthy life expectancy ranges from 57.9 to 74.9 years among countries. The prevalence of wasting in children under 5 years of age ranges from 1% to 13.5%, and stunting from 2.5% to 43.8%. Access to improved water ranges from 64% to 100%, and access to improved sanitation from 42% to 100%. The population using solid fuels (biomass or coal) for cooking and heating ranges from less than 5% to greater than 95%. Implementation of the SDGs will help close these gaps.

Droughts, floods, extreme temperatures and storms have caused more than a quarter million deaths over the past three decades. These conditions have affected about 3.4 billion people and cost more than $500 billion in Forum countries. An expected increase in the frequency of these events, coupled with climate change, will only exacerbate this trend. The commitments made under the Paris Agreement should reduce emissions, providing a major source of hope for reducing air pollution-related death and illness.

The report draws four main conclusions. First, we need to reduce inequalities within and between countries, in the spirit of leaving no one behind. Second, we are increasingly affected by climate and environmental change, which threatens our achievements, and therefore we urgently need to assess the adaptation options we have, even as we pursue decarbonization. Third, we can make good progress by focusing on the SDGs with the understanding that they all converge on health; addressing their interlinkages is a good approach to protect and promote health. Fourth, a core indicator set to monitor performance and progress is required. This report is a start in this direction.

Shin Young-soo, MD, Ph.D.
WHO Regional Director
for the Western Pacific

Dr Poonam Khetrapal Singh
WHO Regional Director
for South-East Asia

Dr Dechen Tsering
UN Environment Regional Director
for Asia and the Pacific

ACKNOWLEDGEMENTS

This report was prepared by the Secretariat of the Asia-Pacific Regional Forum on Environment and Health: the World Health Organization (WHO) Regional Office for South-East Asia; the WHO Regional Office for the Western Pacific; and the Regional Office for Asia and the Pacific of the United Nations Environment Programme (UN Environment). The lead author was Carlos Corvalan with technical contributions from: Susan Mercado, Nasir Hassan, Rokho Kim, Lesley Onyon, Kakuko Nagatani-Yoshida, Katrin Engelhardt, Sangjin Lee and Jungsub Yeom. WHO and UN Environment are also grateful to country representatives who attended the Regional Forum for valuable comments that improved the report.

ABBREVIATIONS

ASEAN	Association of Southeast Asian Nations
CO_2	carbon dioxide
COP	Conference of the Parties
COPD	chronic obstructive pulmonary disease
CRED	Centre for Research on the Epidemiology of Disasters
DALY	disability-adjusted life year
GNI	gross national income
HDI	Human Development Index
INDC	Intended Nationally Determined Contribution
JMP	WHO/UNICEF Joint Monitoring Programme for Water Supply and Sanitation
LPG	liquefied petroleum gas
MDG	Millennium Development Goal
NEHAP	National Environmental Health Action Plan
PM	particulate matter
SDG	Sustainable Development Goal
UN	United Nations
UNDP	United Nations Development Programme
UNEP ROAP	United Nations Environment Programme Regional Office for Asia and the Pacific
UN-Habitat	United Nations Human Settlements Programme
UNICEF	United Nations Children's Fund
WHO	World Health Organization

"...through dialogue, sharing of information and collaboration...
we can transform our lives, our health, and our environment to ensure the well-being of current generations and protect future generations from disasters..."
Manila Declaration 2016
© WHO

INTRODUCTION

This report is a summary of environment and health advances and challenges in the 14 countries that comprise the Asia-Pacific Regional Forum on Environment and Health in Southeast and East Asian Countries: Brunei Darussalam, Cambodia, China, Indonesia, Japan, the Lao People's Democratic Republic, Malaysia, Mongolia, Myanmar, the Philippines, the Republic of Korea, Singapore, Thailand and Viet Nam. The report is based on country profiles submitted by Forum member countries in response to a questionnaire and recent statistics from the World Health Organization (WHO) and other United Nations agencies, in the context of sustainable development and the Sustainable Development Goals (SDGs). The SDGs were launched at the Rio+20 conference in 2012 and agreed upon by heads of state at the United Nations General Assembly in 2015 (United Nations, 2015a). They are a commitment to tackle the world's most pressing development issues by 2030. In the three years since the previous Ministerial Regional Forum on Environment and Health, the SDG targets and indicators have been globally endorsed. There are 17 goals and 169 targets, and health will benefit from actions on many of these (Fig. 1).

Development patterns in the Republic of Korea

The Republic of Korea, once known as one of the world's poorest agrarian societies, has undertaken economic development in earnest since 1962. In less than four decades, the Republic of Korea has achieved what has become known as the "economic miracle on the Han River (a river that runs through Seoul)," an incredible process that dramatically transformed the Korean economy while marking a turning point in the country's history. An outward-oriented economic development strategy, which used exports as the engine of growth, contributed greatly to the radical economic transformation. Based on this strategy, many successful development programmes have been implemented. As a result, from 1962 to 2014, gross national income (GNI) increased from US$ 2.3 billion to US$ 1410.4 billion. Health status has also improved substantially. Life expectancy at birth was 66.1 years in 1980 and 81.9 years in 2014, an increase of nearly 16 years of life in a period of 34 years.

Sources: WHO, Environmental Health Country Report at the Regional Forum Meeting, 2016; UNDP, (2015a).

Fig. 1 The Sustainable Development Goals in relation to health and well-being

Source: WHO, (2016a.)

The 14 Forum countries have a combined population of around 2.2 billion people. They represent, therefore, an important fraction of the world's population – approximately 30% – and 58% of the combined population of WHO's South-East Asia and Western Pacific regions. Forum countries are not homogeneous. They vary greatly in demographic characteristics, environmental risks and health status. For example, countries range in size from 423 000 people (Brunei Darussalam) to over 1.38 billion (China); the proportion of the population using improved drinking water sources ranges from 75% to 100%; and countries range in life expectancy from around 66 to 84 years, a difference of 18 years. All countries, however, have made important advances in key indicators.

This can be best appreciated in the steady improvement by all countries in human development as measured by the Human Development Index (HDI). In 1990, six of the 14 countries had an HDI ranked as "low", and only one ranked "very high". In 2015, only one country remains with a low HDI (although it is very close to the top of the category) and four are ranked as having a very high HDI (Fig. 2).

Fig. 2. Human Development Index in Forum countries, 1990–2014

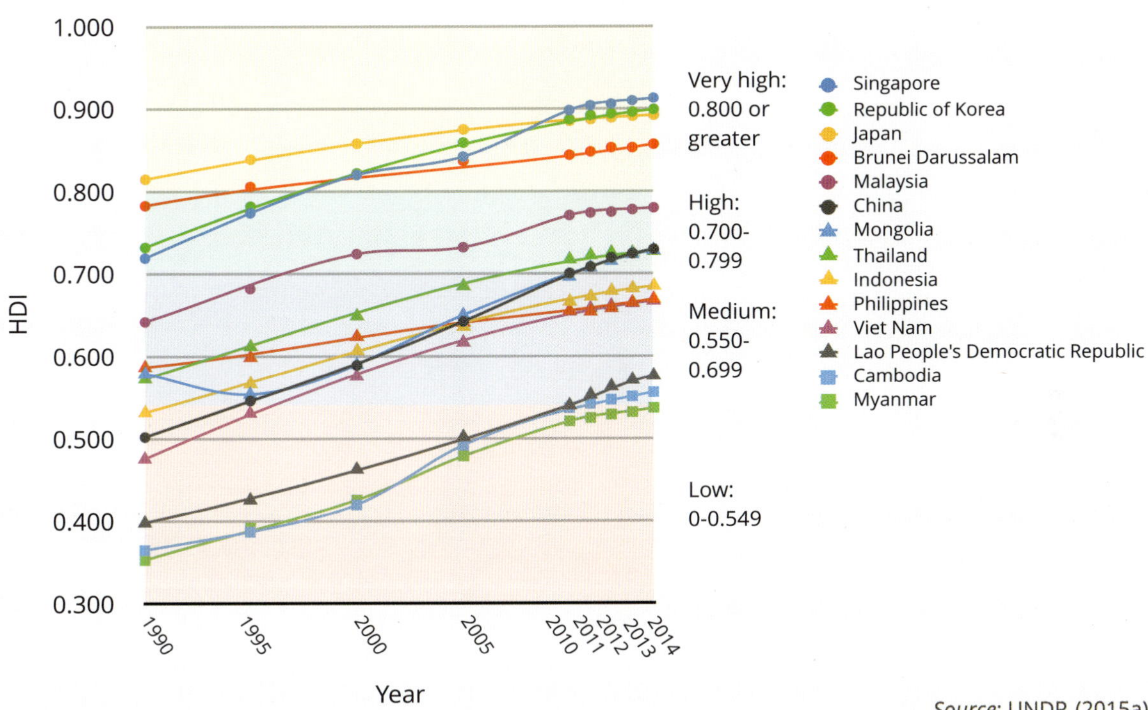

Source: UNDP, (2015a).

Thailand, a happy society with equity, fairness and resilience

The Eleventh National Economic and Social Development Plan (2012–2016) of Thailand envisions a "Happy society with equity, fairness and resilience". The objectives of the national strategy have explicit environmental goals which would result in positive health outcomes: (i) to promote a fair and peaceful society; (ii) to increase the potential of all Thais based on a holistic approach that enables physical, mental, intellectual, emotional, ethical and moral development through social institutions; (iii) to develop an efficient and sustainable economy by upgrading production and services based on technology, innovation and creativity using effective regional links, by improving food and energy security, and by upgrading eco-friendly production and consumption towards a low-carbon society; and (iv) to preserve natural resources and the environment so they are sufficient to maintain ecological balance and a secure foundation for development.

Source: WHO, Environmental Health Country Report at the Regional Forum Meeting, 2016.

THE BURDEN OF DISEASE FROM ENVIRONMENTAL RISKS

In 2016, WHO launched the report *Preventing Disease through Healthy Environments: a Global Assessment of the Burden of Disease from Environmental Factors*. The report stated that 12.6 million global deaths, or 23%, can be attributed to modifiable environmental risk factors. In terms of burden of disease, the fraction is 22% (as measured in disability-adjusted life years, or DALYs) (WHO, 2016a). The 14 Forum countries make a substantial contribution to the environmental burden of disease: over 4 million deaths (32% of the global total).

Globally, 12.6 million deaths can be prevented through environmental interventions, and over 4 million in Forum countries alone.

Of these 4 million deaths, nearly 3.35 million are from noncommunicable diseases; 487 000 deaths or 25% are from injuries; and 190 000 deaths or 7.6% are the result of infectious, parasitic, neonatal and nutritional conditions. In terms of DALYs, the 14 Forum countries combined account for 24% of the global environmental burden of disease (Fig. 3).

Preventing disease through healthy environments – a global assessment of the burden of disease from environmental risks

Environmental risks to health can be defined as "all the physical, chemical and biological factors external to a person, and all related behaviours, but excluding those natural environments that cannot reasonably be modified." Focusing on the part of the environment which can reasonably be modified, the WHO study reviewed 133 diseases or injuries, or their groupings and found that 101 had significant links with the environment, of which 92 were quantified. The study estimated that in 2012, 12.6 million deaths globally, representing 23% of all deaths, were attributable to the environment. When accounting for both death and disability, the fraction of the global burden of disease due to the environment is 22%. In children under 5, up to 26% of all deaths could be prevented, if environmental risks were removed.

Source: WHO, (2016b).

Fig. 3. Deaths and burden of disease (DALYs) from modifiable environmental risks in Forum countries, 2012

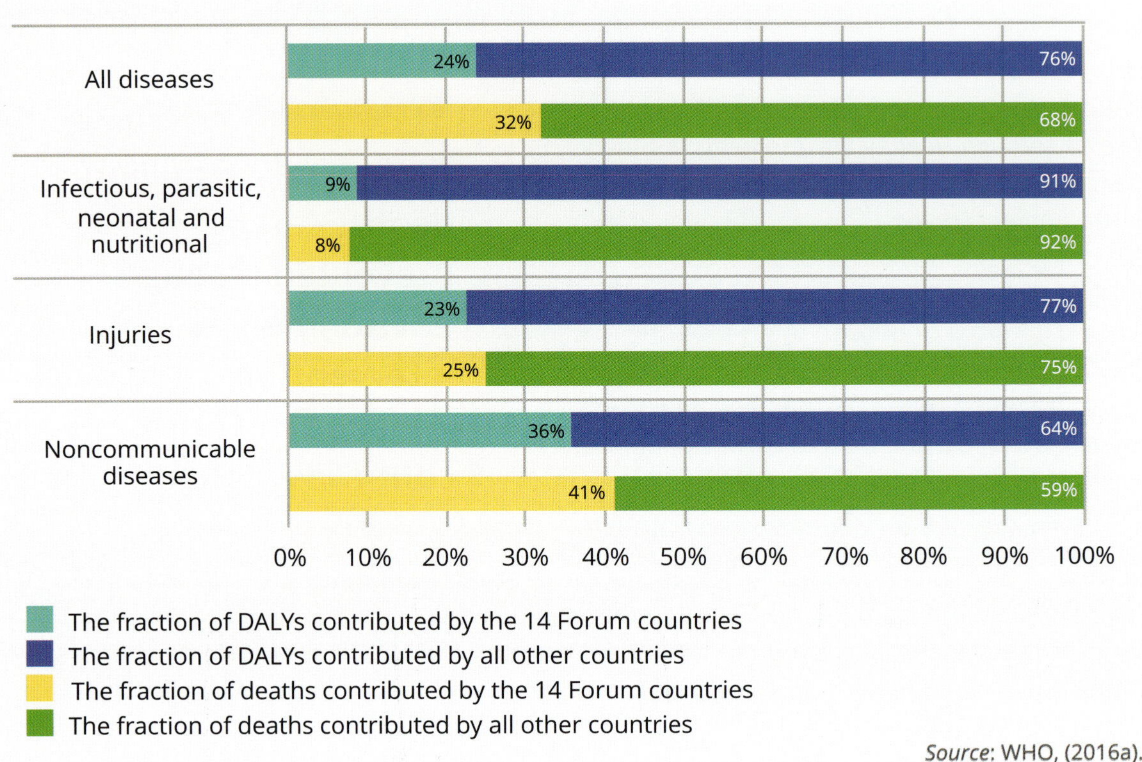

Source: WHO, (2016a).

In all countries, noncommunicable diseases are the biggest killer associated with environmental risks. Air pollution is largely responsible for this. Deaths from infectious, parasitic, neonatal and nutritional conditions resulting from environmental factors are still a tremendous challenge in less developed countries. Availability of clean water would greatly help to address these diseases. Injuries are common in nearly all countries and these include several risks related to housing and the built environment. Workplace risk contributes significantly to all three categories. Fig. 4 shows the age-standardized death rates (per 100 000) from modifiable environmental risks for the same three categories for each of the Forum countries.

Fig. 4. Age-standardized deaths from modifiable environmental risks, 2012

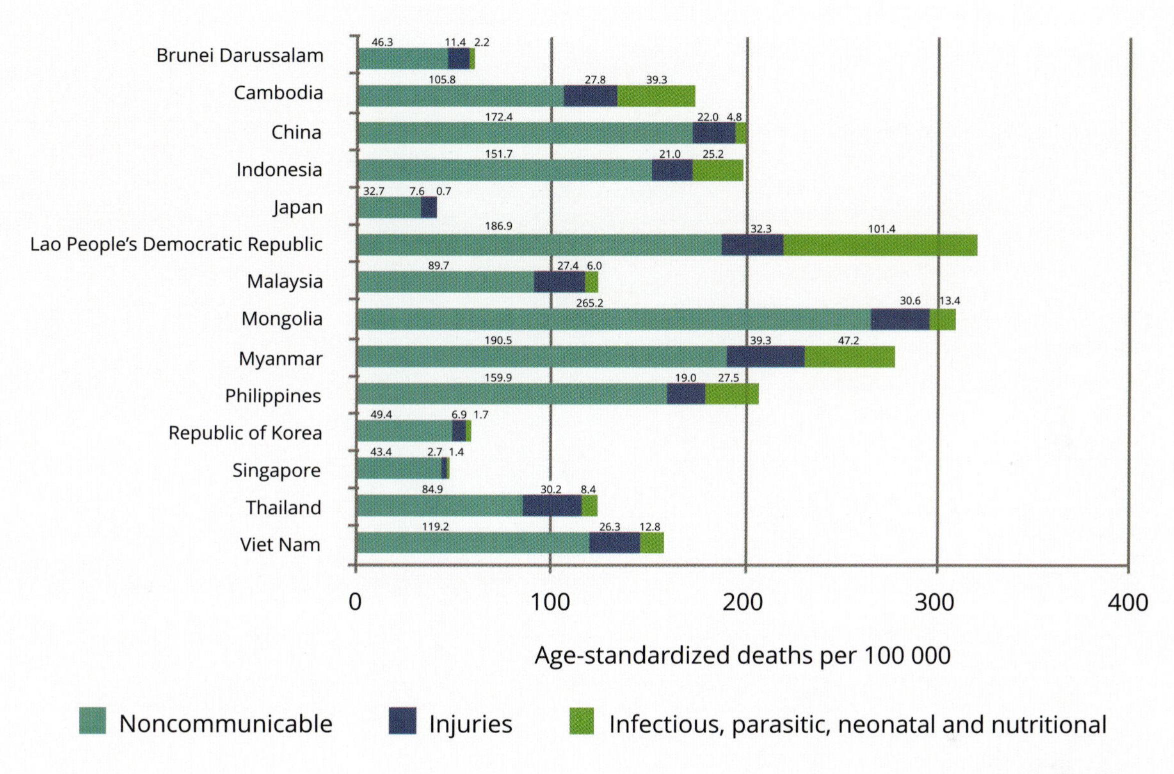

Source: WHO, (2016a).

ENVIRONMENT AND HEALTH IN THE CONTEXT OF THE SDGs

The 17 SDGs are interconnected, and they all contribute, directly or indirectly, to promoting and protecting health. This report analyses the 14 Forum countries in the context of the following SDGs (United Nations, 2015a):

GOAL 2
End hunger, achieve food security and improved nutrition and promote sustainable agriculture

GOAL 3
Ensure healthy lives and promote well-being for all at all ages

GOAL 6
Ensure availability and sustainable management of water and sanitation for all

GOAL 7
Ensure access to affordable, reliable, sustainable and modern energy for all

GOAL 11
Make cities and human settlements inclusive, safe, resilient and sustainable

GOAL 13
Take urgent action to combat climate change and its impacts

For each SDG, the report focuses on specific targets that have a link to health. These SDGs and targets were chosen because they best reflect the relation to specific targets under SDG 3 and the topics addressed in the Country Profiles. Food security and nutrition, water and sanitation, energy sources, cities and human settlements, and climate change are all important environmental determinants of health.

The selected SDGs are also interlinked. Human settlements, for example, need access to water, sanitation and energy. Energy is needed for food production and in many settlements, crop waste and animal dung are burned as fuel. Climate change is not only a threat to health directly, but can adversely affect life in cities and hamper agriculture and food production, and availability and access to water. It is an opportunity to review our relationship to fossil fuels as the primary source of energy, with all of their consequences for health. Indeed, the challenge is to turn these linkages and impacts into possibilities and positive outcomes for health and well-being.

Health and sustainable development

"We recognize that health is a precondition for and an outcome and indicator of all three dimensions of sustainable development. We understand the goals of sustainable development can only be achieved in the absence of a high prevalence of debilitating communicable and noncommunicable diseases, and where populations can reach a state of physical, mental and social well-being. We are convinced that action on the social and environmental determinants of health, both for the poor and the vulnerable and for the entire population, is important to create inclusive, equitable, economically productive and healthy societies."

Source: United Nations, (2012).

END HUNGER, ACHIEVE FOOD SECURITY AND IMPROVED NUTRITION AND PROMOTE SUSTAINABLE AGRICULTURE (SDG 2)

Access to safe and nutritious food sets the foundation for optimal health and development, particularly for children and mothers. SDG 2 addresses sustainable and resilient food production, for which access to arable land, grazing fields and water is essential. In 2015, there were 5.9 million deaths in children under 5, about 45% of which had malnutrition as an underlying contributing factor by making children more vulnerable to severe diseases (WHO, 2016c).

SDG target 2.2 specifically states: by 2030, end all forms of malnutrition, including achieving, by 2025, the internationally agreed targets on stunting and wasting in children under 5 years of age, and address the nutritional needs of adolescent girls, pregnant and lactating women and older persons. WHO Member States endorsed six Global Nutrition Targets 2025 at the World Health Assembly in 2012.

Wasting and overweight in children coexist in many countries. In Forum countries, the prevalence of wasting ranges from 1% to 13.5%, and overweight from 1% to 11.5%.

Japan's Food Safety Commission

The Food Safety Commission, which reports directly to the Cabinet, was established to protect the health of the people by:

- conducting risk assessments on food in a scientific, independent and fair manner, and making recommendations to relevant ministries based upon the results from the risk assessment;
- implementing risk communication practices among stakeholders, such as consumers and food-related businesses; and
- responding to foodborne accidents and emergencies.

Source: WHO, Environmental Health Country Report at the Regional Forum Meeting, 2016.

They provide concrete goals to measure progress towards ending malnutrition in all its forms. The United Nations General Assembly proclaimed the UN Decade of Action on Nutrition 2016–2025, further emphasizing the relevance of improving nutrition for sustainable development. Data are available for 13 of the 14 countries on stunting (chronic undernutrition) and wasting (acute undernutrition) and overweight.

Key facts on food safety

- Access to sufficient amounts of safe and nutritious food is key to sustaining life and promoting good health.
- Unsafe food containing harmful bacteria, viruses, parasites or chemical substances causes more than 200 diseases – ranging from diarrhoea to cancers.
- An estimated 600 million – almost 1 in 10 people in the world – fall ill after eating contaminated food and 420 000 die every year, resulting in the loss of 33 million healthy life years (DALYs).
- Children under 5 years of age carry 40% of the foodborne disease burden, with 125 000 deaths every year.
- Diarrhoeal diseases are the most common illnesses resulting from the consumption of contaminated food, causing 550 million people to fall ill and 230 000 deaths every year.
- Food safety, nutrition and food security are inextricably linked. Unsafe food creates a vicious cycle of disease and malnutrition, particularly affecting infants, young children, older people and sick people.
- Foodborne diseases impede socioeconomic development by straining health-care systems and harming national economies, tourism and trade.
- Food supply chains now cross multiple national borders. Good collaboration between governments, producers and consumers helps ensure food safety.

Source: Adapted from WHO, (2015d).

The prevalence of stunting is still very high in some countries. Global nutrition target 1 proposes a 40% reduction in the number of children under 5 who are stunted. Fig. 5 shows the spread of the distribution among the 13 countries for which data are available, indicating a prevalence of stunting ranging from 2.5% to 43.8%, an 18-fold difference.

Fig. 5. Prevalence of stunting in children under 5, 2005–2015

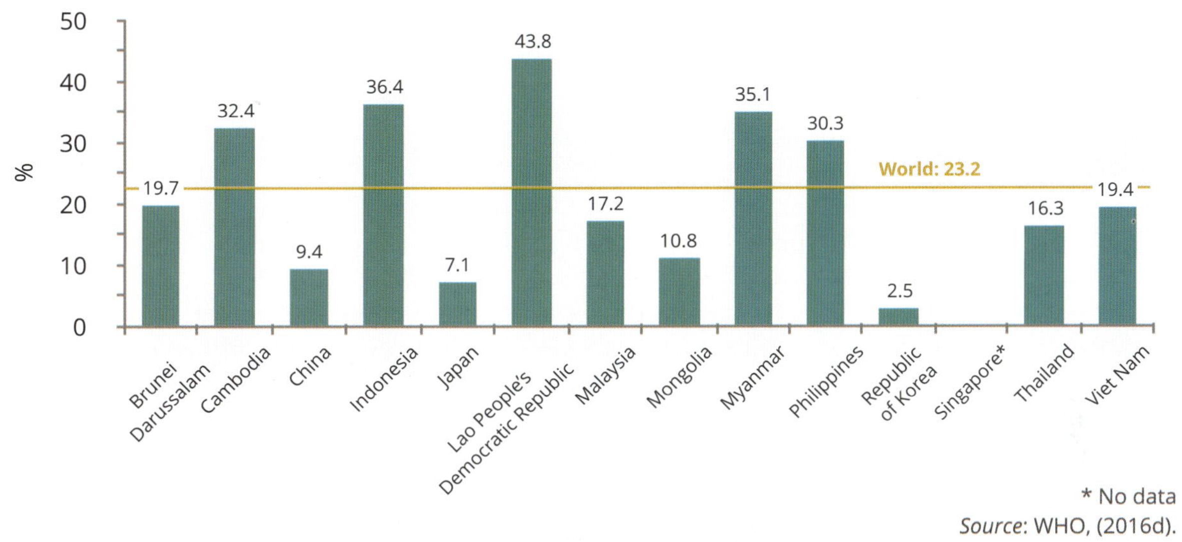

* No data

Source: WHO, (2016d).

Food insecurity in Cambodia

In Cambodia almost two out of three children in the western province of Pursat are chronically undernourished, compared with one in five in Phnom Penh. Meanwhile, Kandal province surrounding the capital has a relatively low stunting (chronic undernutrition) rate, yet over 11% of its children are acutely undernourished.

Child mortality is higher in rural areas, which is linked to high levels of food insecurity. Rural children are 1.5 times more likely to die before they reach the age of 5 than their urban counterparts. Improvements are needed in food and nutrition security, access to health care and other resources necessary for survival.

Source: WHO, Environmental Health Country Report at the Regional Forum Meeting, 2016.

Food production in Myanmar

Myanmar is still an agrarian country with 2.1 million hectares of irrigated agricultural area. The sector is expected to grow as part of the government's intensive development programme. Areas of intervention are water and resources development and conservation, irrigation systems development, rural development, agro-industry development and capacity development of relevant agencies.

In addition, development of livestock and fisheries is important for both growth and poverty reduction. Reform strategies for these subsectors will be developed that focus on measures to reduce production costs and improve product quality while ensuring the balanced development of both the small-scale producers and larger enterprises. Special attention is given to minimizing environmental consequences, protecting vulnerable populations and providing capacity-building and livelihood support to local populations who are dependent on the sector.

Source: WHO, Environmental Health Country Report at the Regional Forum Meeting, 2016.

Fig. 6. Prevalence of wasting and overweight in children under 5, 2005–2015

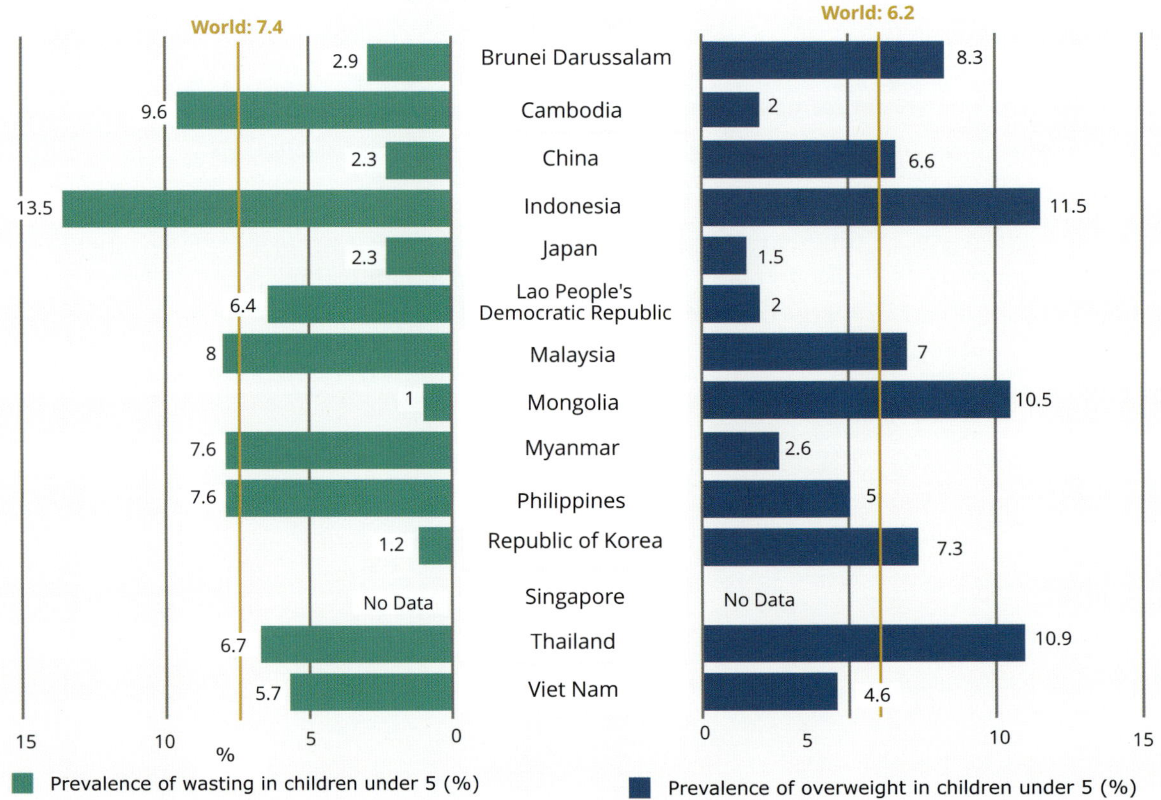

Sources: WHO, (2016d); ASEAN/UNICEF/WHO, (2016).

Global nutrition target 6 aims to reduce and maintain childhood wasting to less than 5%. Current prevalence of wasting ranges from 1% to 13.5%, and eight of the 13 countries for which data are available have a prevalence of over 5%. In many countries wasting occurs in parallel to overweight. Global nutrition target 4 aims for no increase in childhood overweight. Prevalence of overweight in the 13 countries with data available ranges from 1.5% to 11.5% (Fig. 6).

ENSURE AVAILABILITY AND SUSTAINABLE MANAGEMENT OF WATER AND SANITATION FOR ALL (SDG 6)

SDG 6 has eight interlinked targets that address access to drinking water, adequate sanitation, improved water quality, water scarcity, water resources management, water-related ecosystems, capacity-building and community participation. Addressing all these targets would have important positive outcomes in achieving health-related targets, including reductions in child mortality and reductions of several communicable diseases.

Access to clean water and safe sanitation practices are effective ways to reduce health impacts, particularly diarrhoeal diseases in children. The WHO/UNICEF Joint Monitoring Programme for Water Supply and Sanitation (JMP) began monitoring the sector in 1990. Data are available for 13 of the 14 Forum countries. SDG target 6.1 is to: by 2030, achieve universal and equitable access to safe and affordable drinking water for all. JMP has been monitoring access to water as part of the Millennium Development Goals (MDGs) process. In its 2015 evaluation, it concluded that the global MDG target for drinking water was met in 2010. This assessment also indicated that of the 14 Forum countries, 11 had met the MDG target for water, one had made moderate progress, and two had no available data to report. Forum countries had access to safe water, which ranged from 23% to 100% in 1990, and from 64% to 100% in 2015. This progress can be seen in Fig. 7. In the Forum countries, as of 2015, 126 million people (or 5.7% of the population of these countries) still lack access to improved drinking-water sources (WHO/UNICEF, 2015b).

In Forum countries, 126 million people lack access to an improved drinking- water source and 506 million lack improved sanitation.

SDG target 6.2 proposes to: by 2030, achieve access to adequate and equitable sanitation and hygiene for all and end open defecation, paying special attention to the needs of women and girls and those in vulnerable situations. JMP has also been monitoring access to sanitation as part of the MDG process and the 2015 evaluation concluded that the global MDG target for sanitation was missed by almost 700 million people. This assessment also indicated that of the 14 Forum countries, nine met the target, three made good progress, one made moderate progress, and one did not report data. Forum countries had access to improved sanitation ranging from 2.9% to 100% in 1990, and from 42% to 100% in 2015. This progress can be seen in Fig. 8. Access to improved sanitation is still lacking for 506 million people in the Forum countries, representing nearly 23% of their combined population (WHO/UNICEF, 2015b).

Water supply and sanitation in Viet Nam

In Viet Nam, urban water supply and sanitation is the responsibility of both the central and provincial governments. Central government agencies are chiefly responsible for policy-making, standards and development. Provincial and local governments are responsible for construction, supervision, operation and maintenance of water supply systems. Almost 1.3 million people, accounting for 80% of the total population in the four project provinces, gained access to improved water sources and 100% of poor households had access to water supply and sanitation services. Households received access to low-interest loans to build or rehabilitate more than 48 000 hygienic toilets and sanitation facilities, increasing the proportion of households with hygienic toilets from 25% to 87%. More than 650 public sanitation facilities were built for local schools and health stations. About 90% of households were reported to be highly satisfied with services.

Source: WHO, Environmental Health Country Report at the Regional Forum Meeting, 2016.

Water scarcity is a concern for many countries and communities and is a problem likely to worsen because of unsustainable water withdrawal and climate change. It is estimated that by 2025, half of the world's population will be living in water-stressed areas (WHO, 2015c). Freshwater withdrawal (as a percentage of total renewable water resources per year for 2007–2011) varies substantially among Forum countries; it ranges from 1% or less in Cambodia and in the Lao People's Democratic Republic, to 32% in Singapore and nearly 37% in the Republic of Korea (UNDP, 2015b).

Fig. 7. Trends in Forum countries in total access to improved water, 1990–2015

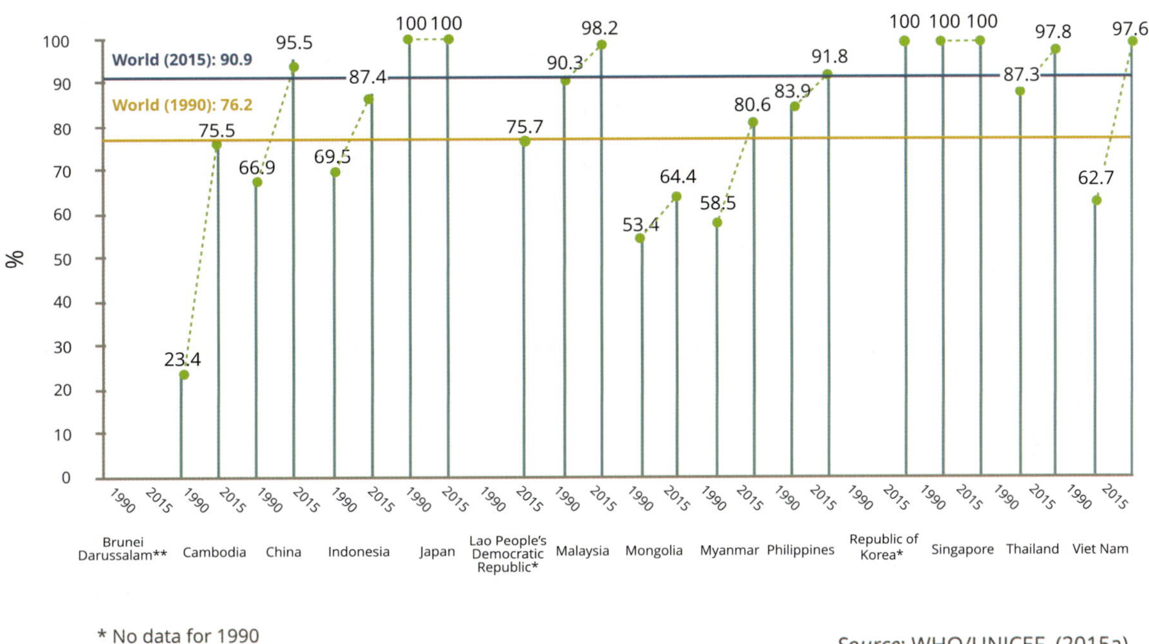

* No data for 1990
** No data for both

Source: WHO/UNICEF, (2015a).

Fig. 8. Trends in Forum countries in total access to improved sanitation, 1990–2015

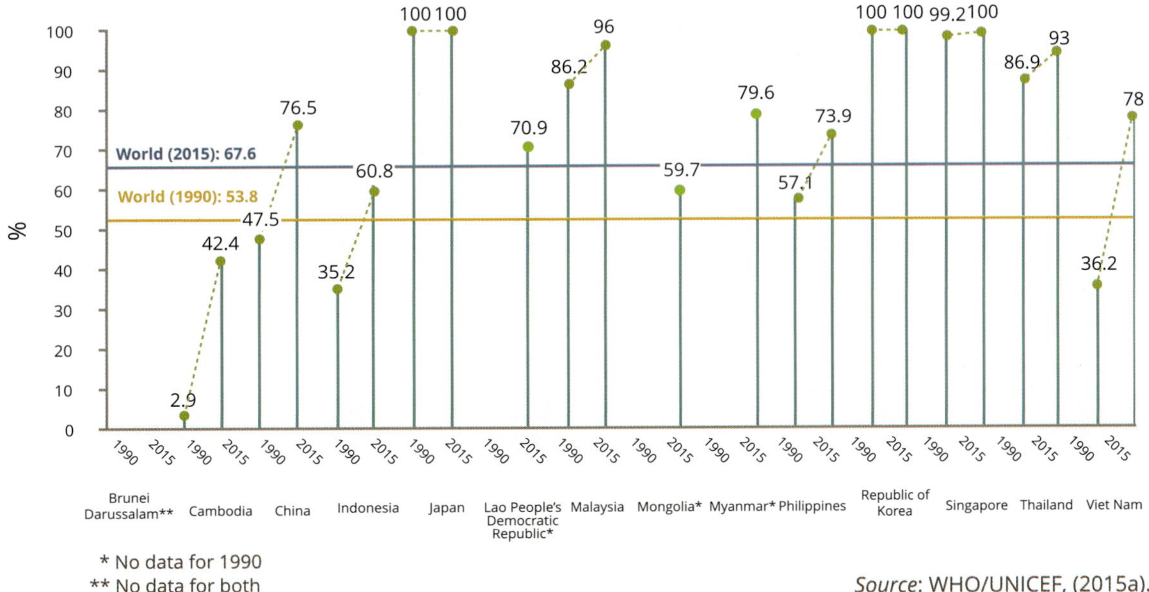

* No data for 1990
** No data for both

Source: WHO/UNICEF, (2015a).

Reducing water chemical pollution in China

China has increased access to drinking water for households and is making efforts to strengthen controls in industrial production to reduce water pollution. Polluting industries are being required to meet new national requirements by the end of 2016. Many provinces are planning to relocate more than 1000 chemical plants away from populated regions, and to persuade companies causing water pollution to upgrade to cleaner technology. Water pollution is concentrated in several major industries such as papermaking, food processing, chemicals and textiles, which account for half the total water pollutants nationwide. Many of these industries are found along large rivers. Industrial zones will be required to establish sewage processing plants.

Source: WHO, Environmental Health Country Report at the Regional Forum Meeting, 2016.

ENSURE ACCESS TO AFFORDABLE, RELIABLE, SUSTAINABLE AND MODERN ENERGY FOR ALL (SDG 7)

Availability and access to clean energy is a great challenge, particularly for the poor. SDG target 7.1 proposes: by 2030, ensure universal access to affordable, reliable and modern energy services. Burning biomass or coal, the only accessible fuel for many poor communities, is neither affordable nor reliable or modern. WHO data for 2013 show that the population using solid fuels in the 14 Forum countries ranges from less than 5% to over 95%; therefore, there is still a long way to go towards achieving this target (Fig. 9).

In the 14 Forum countries, nearly 1.85 million people die from household air pollution each year, 43% of the global total.

Fig. 9. Solid fuel use

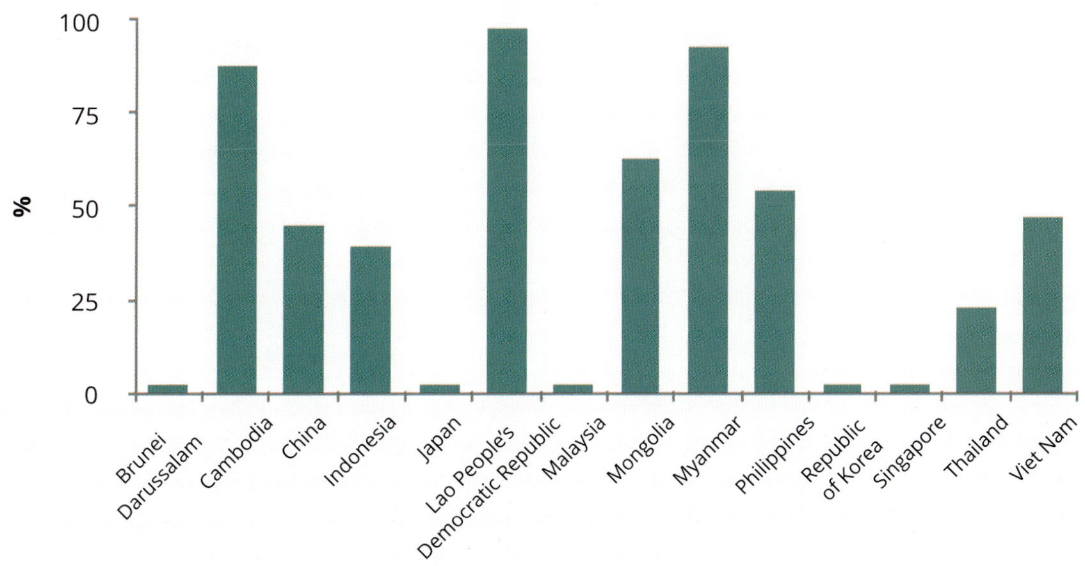

Source: WHO, (2013).

According to WHO, 4.3 million people a year die from exposure to household air pollution, mostly from burning biomass (wood, crop waste and animal dung) and coal for cooking and heating. Of these deaths, 12% are due to pneumonia, 34% to stroke, 26% to ischaemic heart disease, 22% to chronic obstructive pulmonary disease (COPD) and 6% to lung cancer (WHO, 2016e). In the 14 Forum countries, nearly 1.85 million people die from household air pollution each year (43% of the global total), based on 2012 estimates (Fig. 10).

Fig. 10. Attributable deaths from household air pollution

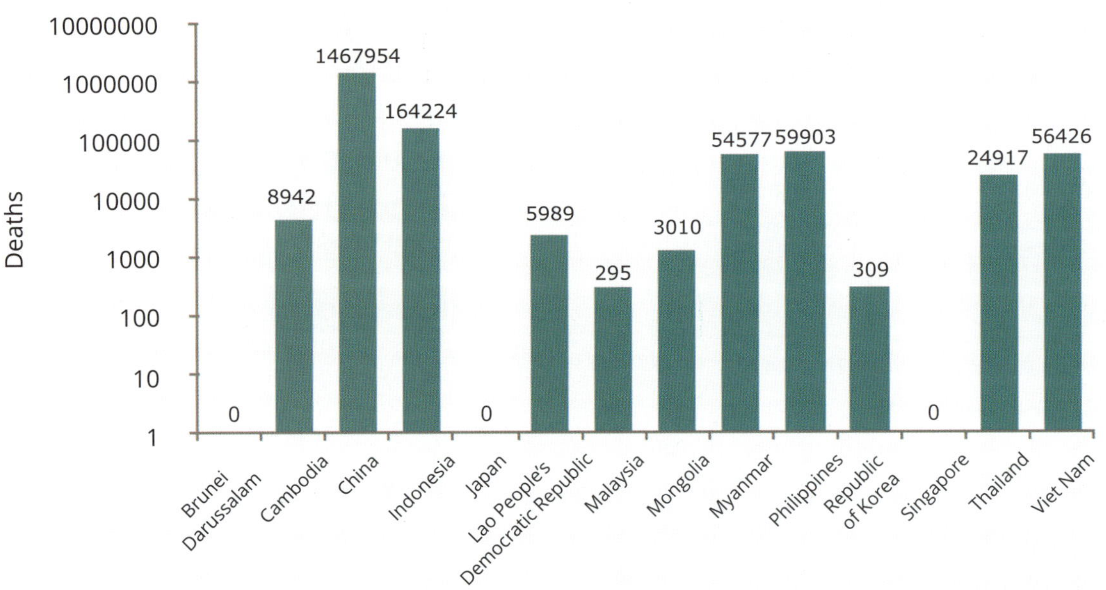

Source: WHO, (2014).

Increasing use of clean fuel in Indonesia

Since 2007, households in Indonesia using natural gas or liquefied petroleum gas (LPG) for cooking significantly increased as a result of the gradual kerosene-to-LPG conversion programme launched by the Government in order to reduce dependency on petroleum. In 2014, about 62% of the total population relied on natural gas or LPG for cooking or heating, followed by firewood (almost 30%), kerosene (5%), electricity (0.6%), charcoal (0.3%) and others (2.4%). Household use of firewood for cooking is still prevalent in the largely rural provinces of Nusa Tenggara, Sulawesi, Maluku and Papua.

Source: WHO, Environmental Health Country Report at the Regional Forum Meeting, 2016.

Household energy in Myanmar

From the 2014 census, four out of five households in Myanmar use wood or charcoal as the main source of energy for cooking. In urban areas, over half of the households use wood or charcoal, while in the rural areas 80% use wood or charcoal for cooking. This has implications for indoor air pollution due to exposure to smoke during cooking, resulting in adverse health impacts mostly to women and children.

Source: WHO, Environmental Health Country Report at the Regional Forum Meeting, 2016.

Super Cub

MAKE CITIES AND HUMAN SETTLEMENTS INCLUSIVE, SAFE, RESILIENT AND SUSTAINABLE (SDG 11)

Cities are home to 56% of the population in Forum countries, or over 1.2 billion people. Some countries are highly urbanized such as Singapore, Japan and the Republic of Korea, while in others a large fraction of the population live in rural areas, such as in Cambodia, Myanmar and the Lao People's Democratic Republic. However regardless of urban or rural differences, most people live in settlements, whether they are small villages, towns or larger cities. Human settlements can be damaging or promoting and protective of health. The built environment, whether large or small, is therefore an important determinant of health. Of the 30 largest cities in the world in 2015, 10 are in the Forum countries, with six in China, two in Japan, and one each in the Philippines and Indonesia, with a combined population of 173 million (United Nations, 2014).

Of the 30 largest cities in the world in 2015, 10 are in Forum countries with a combined population of 173 million.

SDG target 11.1 proposes to: by 2030, ensure access for all to adequate, safe and affordable housing and basic services and upgrade slums. The challenges to achieve this target are enormous. According to the United Nations Human Settlements Programme (UN-Habitat), each day 120 000 people are added to the population of Asian cities, which would require the construction of at least 20 000 new dwellings – and their supporting infrastructure – every day. Estimates for 2014 for nine of the Forum countries indicate there are 265 million people living in slums (United Nations, 2015b). For many of these settlers, lack of access to clean water, sanitation and clean energy is an important environmental determinant of health.

Poverty and household air pollution in the Philippines

One basic service that is often missing is clean energy for the poor. Air pollution in and around the home is largely a result of the burning of solid fuels (biomass or coal) for cooking. Women and children are at greater risk for disease from household air pollution. Consequently, household air pollution is responsible for a larger proportion of the total number of deaths from ischaemic heart disease, stroke, lung cancer and COPD in women than men. In the Philippines, 46% of an estimated 12 700 child deaths due to acute lower respiratory infections are attributable to household air pollution (WHO, 2012).

Source: WHO, (2015a).

Forum countries are also highly affected by natural disasters. SDG target 11.5 proposes to: by 2030, significantly reduce the number of deaths and the number of people affected and substantially decrease the direct economic losses relative to global gross domestic product caused by disasters, including water-related disasters, with a focus on protecting the poor and people in vulnerable situations.

Major storms were registered in 12 Forum countries, with 668 occurrences from 1990 to 2015. The database registered over 187 000 deaths, nearly 263 000 injured persons, 197 000 left homeless, and a total of over 600 million people affected (some more than once). According to the Centre for Research on the Epidemiology of Disasters (CRED) the combined economic loss for all countries was close to US$ 179.50 billion.

Damaging earthquakes were registered in seven Forum countries, with 238 occurring between 1990 and 2015. They resulted in over 308 000 deaths and close to 722 000 injuries. Nearly 5.9 million people were left homeless and a total of over 89.3 million were affected. Economic losses are estimated at close to US$ 474 billion (CRED, 2016).

Droughts were registered in 10 countries. From 1990 to 2015, there were 61 prolonged dry spells, over 2800 deaths, and 494 million people affected. The total damage is estimated at a cost of over US$ 474 billion (CRED, 2016).

Floods were recorded in 12 countries. From 1990 to 2015, there were 708 flooding events, nearly 46 000 deaths, over a million people injured, nearly 40.3 million left homeless, and over 1.9 billion affected. The total damage is estimated at US$ 285.5 billion (CRED, 2016).

In summary, disasters are a recurrent problem in Forum countries. Earthquakes are the most deadly and most expensive of the disasters analysed; however, they tend to be concentrated in a smaller geographical area than other kinds of disasters and, therefore, have the lowest total number of affected persons. Floods affected more people than any other disaster and were the second-costliest type of disaster.

Water resources and flooding in the Lao People's Democratic Republic

The Lao People's Democratic Republic possesses a large per capita volume of internal renewable water resources. Around 90% of the country is in the Mekong River basin, and its Lao tributaries contribute 35% of the annual flow of the Mekong River. About 75% of the rainfall occurs during the rainy season, and water level in the Mekong River may fluctuate by up to 20 metres between wet and dry seasons. Flooding is therefore a permanent concern for the country. There are six important flood-prone areas, five in the Mekong River basin and one in the Sekong River basin. Since 1990, there have been 18 reported floods with 148 deaths, nearly 3.9 million affected (many more than once), and an estimated US$ 154 million in damage.

Sources: WHO, Environmental Health Country Report at the Regional Forum Meeting, 2016; CRED, (2016).

The consequences of inadequate waste collection in the Philippines

The Philippines generates 30 000 tons of garbage every day. Metro Manila alone produces 8000 tonnes per day, of which 70% is collected. For the entire country, only 50% of the waste generated is collected. Uncollected refuse ends up mostly in rivers, swamps and other water bodies, clogging the drainage systems and causing floods and pollution of major water bodies.

Source: WHO, Environmental Health Country Report at the Regional Forum Meeting, 2016.

Waste generation in Singapore

Waste generation is a global problem. Left unchecked, it can rapidly contaminate large bodies of land and water and has diverse health impacts. In 2014, Singapore produced enough incinerable solid waste to fill 1030 football fields to the height of an average person. This amount would be significantly higher if Singapore did not recycle an almost equivalent amount of waste. Singapore's output of solid waste has increased significantly over the years: from 1260 tonnes per day in 1970, to a high of 8338 tonnes per day in 2014.

Source: WHO, Environmental Health Country Report at the Regional Forum Meeting, 2016.

The Sendai Framework for Disaster Risk Reduction 2015–2030 warns that as many disasters are exacerbated by climate change, and increasing in frequency and intensity, they impede progress towards sustainable development. Therefore, climate change as one important driver of disaster risk must be addressed in order to limit this risk.

SDG target 11.6 is to: by 2030, reduce the adverse per capita environmental impact of cities, including by paying special attention to air quality and municipal and other waste management. Globally, ambient air pollution (measured as particulate matter of less than 2.5 micrometres (µg/m³ or $PM_{2.5}$) is responsible for around 3 million deaths per year (based on 2012 estimates), representing 5.4% of all deaths. Poor outdoor air quality is estimated to cause about 25% of lung cancer deaths, about 17% of respiratory infection deaths, about 15% of ischaemic heart disease and stroke, and 8% of COPD deaths (WHO, 2016f). WHO has an air quality database of nearly 3000 cities in 104 countries. There are 10 Forum countries listed in the database, with a combined total of 298 cities reporting air pollution data. In these cities, annual means of $PM_{2.5}$ range from 10 to 128 µg/m³ (WHO, 2016g). In the Forum countries, data on mean concentration of $PM_{2.5}$ in urban areas combined range from 5 to 59 µg/m³ (Fig. 11). Mortality data are not available for individual countries, but are aggregated by region. For the South-East Asia Region, combined with low- and middle-income countries of the Western Pacific Region, there were a total of 1.9 million deaths in 2012, or approximately 64% of all global ambient air pollution-related deaths (WHO, 2016f).

Fig. 11. Estimated annual mean concentration of fine particulate matter ($PM_{2.5}$) in urban areas (µg/m³)

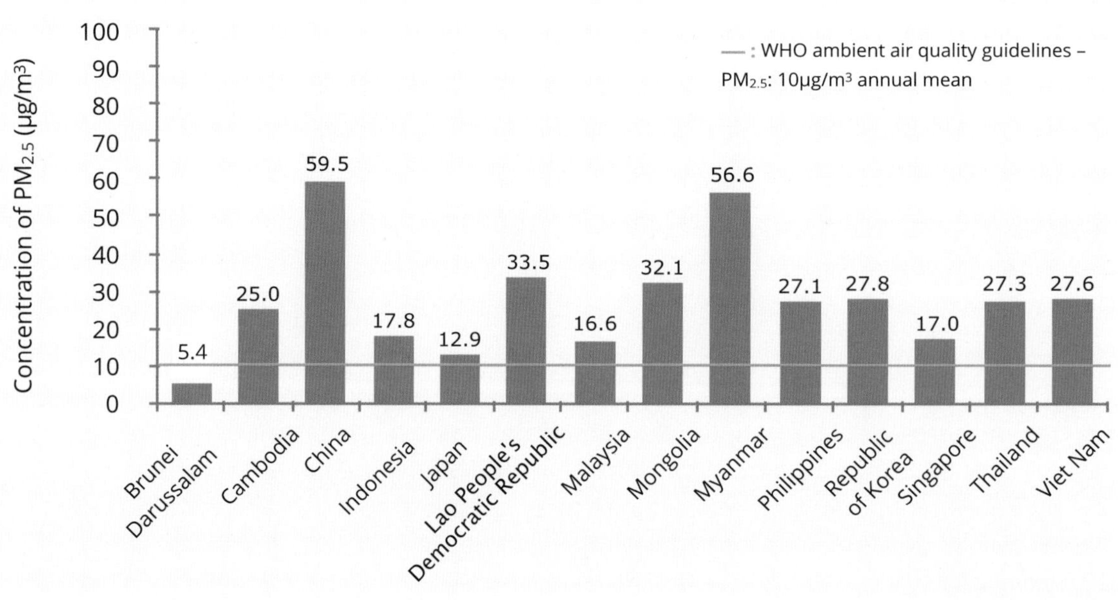

Source: WHO, (2014).

Motor vehicle fleet in Indonesia

Motor vehicles are a source of air pollution and of road injuries and fatalities. Motorcycles contribute to both. In 2014, there were 112.88 million registered vehicles in Indonesia plying the 508 000-kilometre road network, 57% of which was paved. The most common type of vehicle registered was motorcycles at 92.52 million, followed by passenger cars, 12.26 million; trucks, 5.7 million; and public buses, 2.3 million. The provinces in the island of Java recorded the highest number of motorcycle registrations.

Sources: WHO, Environmental Health Country Report at the Regional Forum Meeting, 2016; CRED, (2016).

MAY REKLAMO KA?
ITAWAG SA LTFRB
CEL#:0921-4487777
TEL#:426-25-15

TAKE URGENT ACTION TO COMBAT CLIMATE CHANGE AND ITS IMPACTS (SDG 13)

Climate change is among the greatest threats to health the world faces. Global, regional and country impacts on health include more extreme weather events, increased transmission and spread of infectious diseases, and the impacts on other environmental determinants of health, including clean air and water, and food sufficiency (WHO, 2016h). Forum countries are committed to addressing climate change. Intended Nationally Determined Contributions (INDCs) reflect the climate actions planned by countries as submitted to the United Nations Framework Convention on Climate Change in advance of the Conference of the Parties (COP) held in Paris in December 2015.

SDG target 13.1 aims to: strengthen resilience and adaptive capacity to climate-related hazards and natural disasters in all countries. Forum countries are exposed to climate-related natural disasters regularly and climate change threatens to make these worse. If countries are not fully prepared for current events, the future can only be worse. Preparation is therefore urgent. Building resilience in communities, organizations and government is a necessity.

Taking together climatological (droughts), hydrological (floods) and meteorological (extreme temperatures and storms) disasters, 1577 different events hit Forum countries in the three decades to 2015, with nearly 252 000 deaths and around 3.4 billion people affected. The combined cost over 30 years was more than $500 billion. There has been an increase in the annual number of events and costs, although the number of deaths and total number of affected persons have bucked this trend (Fig. 12) (CRED, 2016). Climate fluctuations influenced by El Niño and La Niña can make specific disasters particularly damaging.

"While health emergencies hit quickly, climate change is a slow-motion disaster. WHO must play a strategic and decisive role not only in adaptation but also in mitigation."

Dr Tedros Adhanom Ghebreyesus,
WHO Director-General

SDG target 13.2 aims to: integrate climate change measures into national policies, strategies and planning. Countries understand the need to make all feasible reductions to emissions of greenhouse gases. The 14 countries vary greatly in their emissions, from 0.2 metric tonnes to 24.0 metric tonnes per capita, based on 2011 data (UNDP, 2015a). Fig. 13 shows emission trends in Forum countries (UNDP, 2015a). As all countries signed the Paris Agreement, emissions reductions are going to be implemented, which as a co-benefit will make an immediate contribution to reducing the burden of disease from air pollution.

Health and the Paris Agreement

The Paris Agreement, adopted on 12 December 2015, marks the beginning of a new era in the global response to climate change. The world now has a global climate agreement – which will have a major public health policy impact as countries take action. As stated in the Agreement, "the right to health" will be central to the actions taken.

The Agreement not only sets ambitious aims to curb greenhouse gas emissions to keep global warming well below 2°C, it also commits countries to strengthen adaptation. This includes implementing plans that should protect human health from the worst impacts of climate change, such as air pollution, heat waves, floods and droughts, and the ongoing degradation of water resources and food security. It commits countries to finance clean and resilient futures in the most vulnerable countries.

Source: WHO, (2016i).

The Lao People's Democratic Republic's vision to address climate change

To secure a future where the Lao People's Democratic Republic is capable of mitigating and adapting to changing climatic conditions in a way that promotes sustainable economic development, reduces poverty, protects public health and safety, enhances the quality of the natural environment, and advances the quality of life for all Lao people.

Source: Lao People's Democratic Republic, (2015).

Fig. 12. Number of climate-related disasters and number of affected persons in Forum countries for 30 years from 1986 to 2015

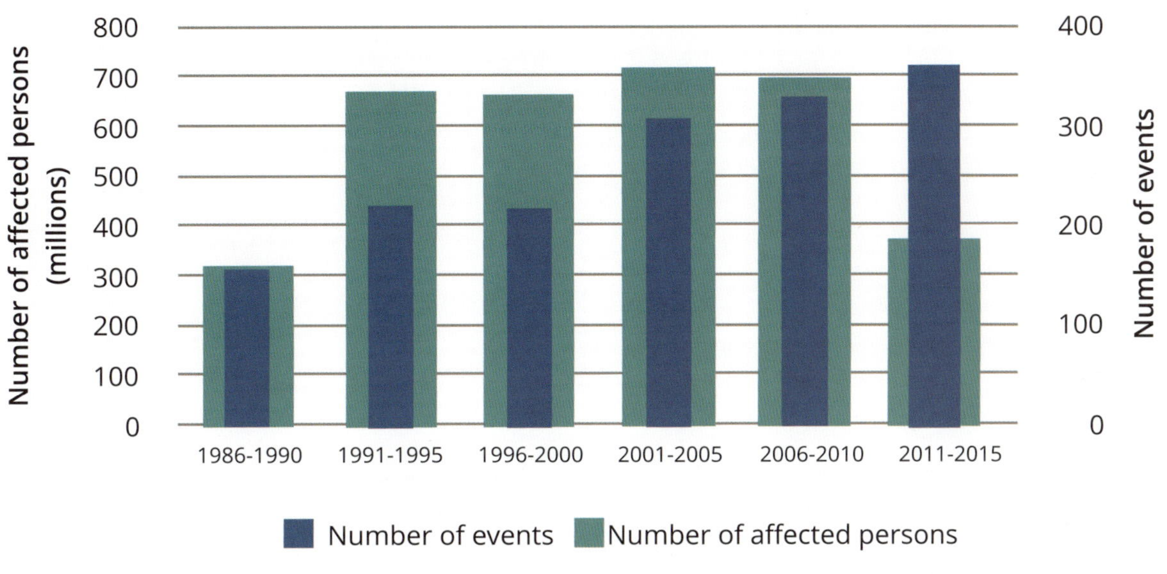

Source: CRED, (2016).

Fig. 13. Per capita carbon dioxide (CO_2) emissions in Forum countries, 1990–2011

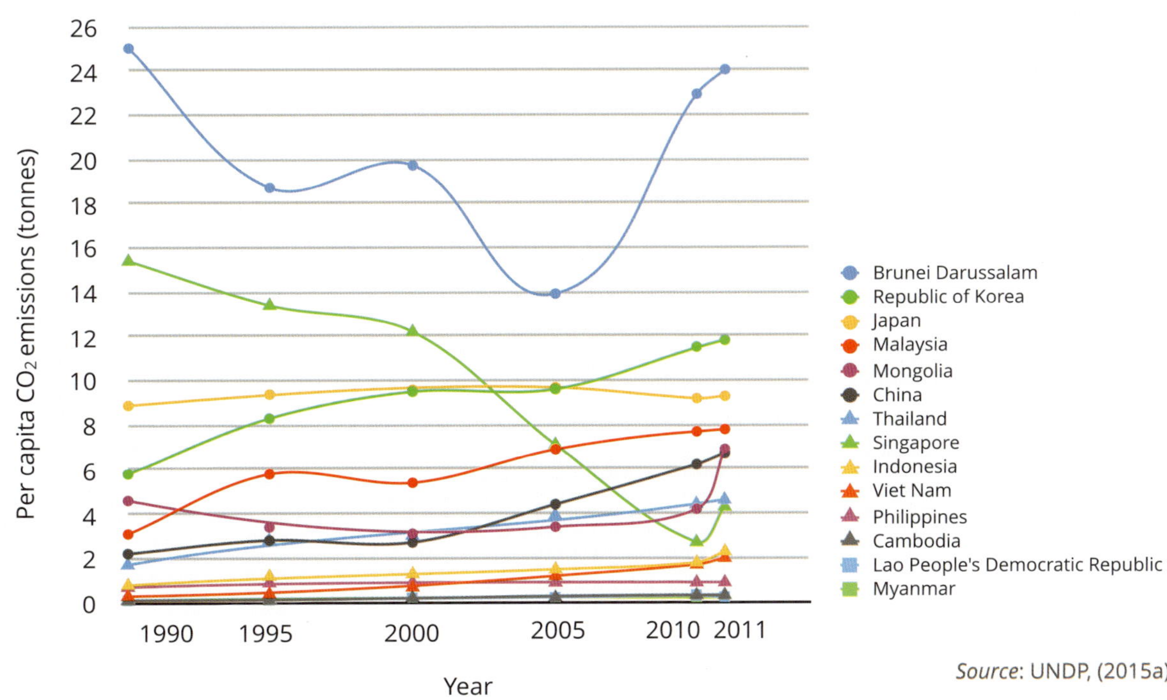

Source: UNDP, (2015a).

Responding to climate change in Malaysia

Malaysia has adopted a National Policy on Climate Change which incorporates health perspectives. Currently Malaysia has a number of policies and plans which are responsive to climate change, such as flood mitigation plans and fire suppression plans. Malaysia is taking steps to address the potential health impacts of climate change by managing the aspects that may affect public health. From time to time, response measures are also being established to avoid situations that will affect or worsen public health due to climate change impacts.

Source: WHO, (2015a).

Extreme weather events in Mongolia

Common extreme weather events in Mongolia include strong windstorms, thunderstorms, heatwaves, droughts and flash floods, in addition to extreme snowfall and a combination of long, cold and dry winter periods, known as *dzud*. Projections are that the frequency and intensity of these events will increase with a number of direct and indirect impacts on human health. Direct impacts include heatwave- and flood-related mortality, but indirect impacts are more likely and more serious due to effects such as the loss of livestock, desertification and other drivers of agricultural failure, as well as increased rates of diarrhoeal diseases following flooding.

Source: WHO, (2015d).

Short-lived climate pollutants

Short-lived climate pollutants such as black carbon, methane and tropospheric ozone – released through inefficient use and burning of biomass and fossil fuels for transport, housing, power production, industry, waste disposal (municipal and agricultural) and forest fires – are responsible for a substantial fraction of global warming as well as air pollution--related deaths and diseases. Since short-lived climate pollutants persist in the atmosphere for weeks or months while CO_2 emissions persist for years, significant reductions of short-lived climate pollutants emissions could result in immediate health benefits and health cost savings, and generate very rapid climate benefits – helping to reduce near-term climate change by as much as 0.5 °C before 2050.

Source: WHO, (2015a).

ENSURE HEALTHY LIVES AND PROMOTE WELL-BEING FOR ALL AT ALL AGES (SDG 3)

Life expectancy at birth has improved in all Forum countries. The gap between the lowest and highest life expectancy among females in the 14 countries was 27 years in 1990, closing to 18.9 years in 2015. For males, the difference was 23.6 years in 1990, and down to 15.2 years in 2015. As expected, the most notable advances were in countries with low life expectancy in 1990. Cambodia, for example, had a gain of 14.9 years for females and 15.5 for males in the 1990–2015 period. Differences between males and females for 2015 range from 9.4 years in Viet Nam, down to 2.8 years for the Lao People's Democratic Republic (Fig. 14). Healthy life expectancy is defined as the average number of years that a person can expect to live in full health, by taking into account years lived in less than full health due to disease and/or injury. In Forum countries, healthy life expectancy ranges from 57.9 to 74.9 years, and on average between 7 and 9 years of healthy life are lost (Fig. 15).

In Forum countries, healthy life expectancy ranges from 57.9 to 74.9 years, and on average between 7 and 9 years of healthy life are lost to disease and injury.

A large fraction of children's deaths are linked to the environment. SDG target 3.2 proposes to: by 2030, end preventable deaths of newborns and children under 5 years of age, with all countries aiming to reduce neonatal mortality to at least as low as 12 per 1000 live births and under-5 mortality to at least as low as 25 per 1000 live births.

According to the study of burden of disease from environmental risks, at the global level, 26% of deaths in children aged 0–4 years are attributable to environmental risks. This figure is higher in the South-East Asia Region at 28%, and in the Western Pacific Region at 27% (excluding Western Pacific high-income countries, this proportion is 29%) (WHO, 2016a). Fig. 16 and Fig. 17 each show under-5 and neonatal mortality rates for the 14 Forum countries, regions and the global estimates for 2015 (WHO, 2016d).

Fig. 14. Changes in life expectancy between 1990 and 2015

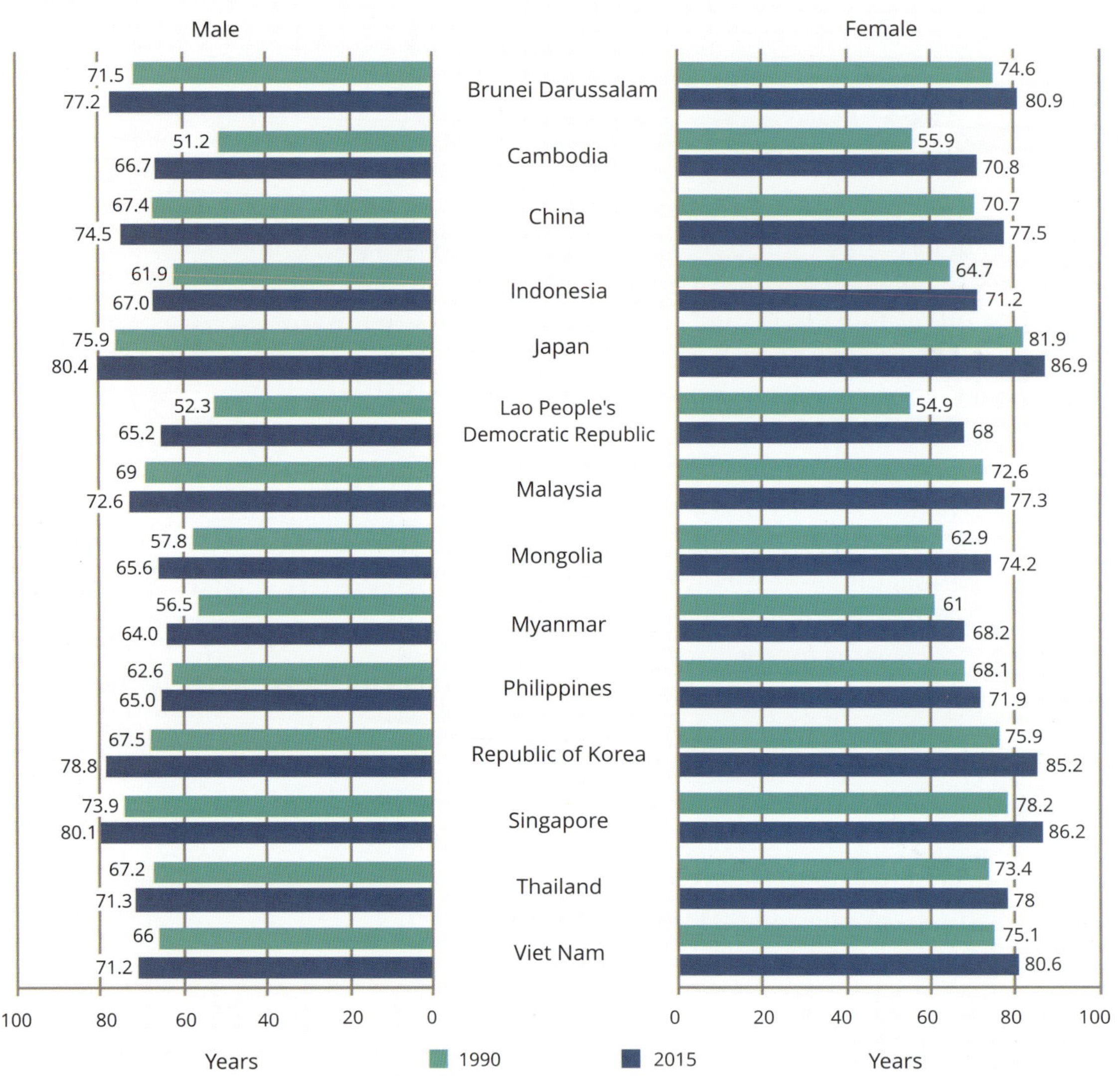

Source: UNDP, (2015a).

Fig. 15. Life expectancy and healthy life expectancy at birth, both sexes, 2015

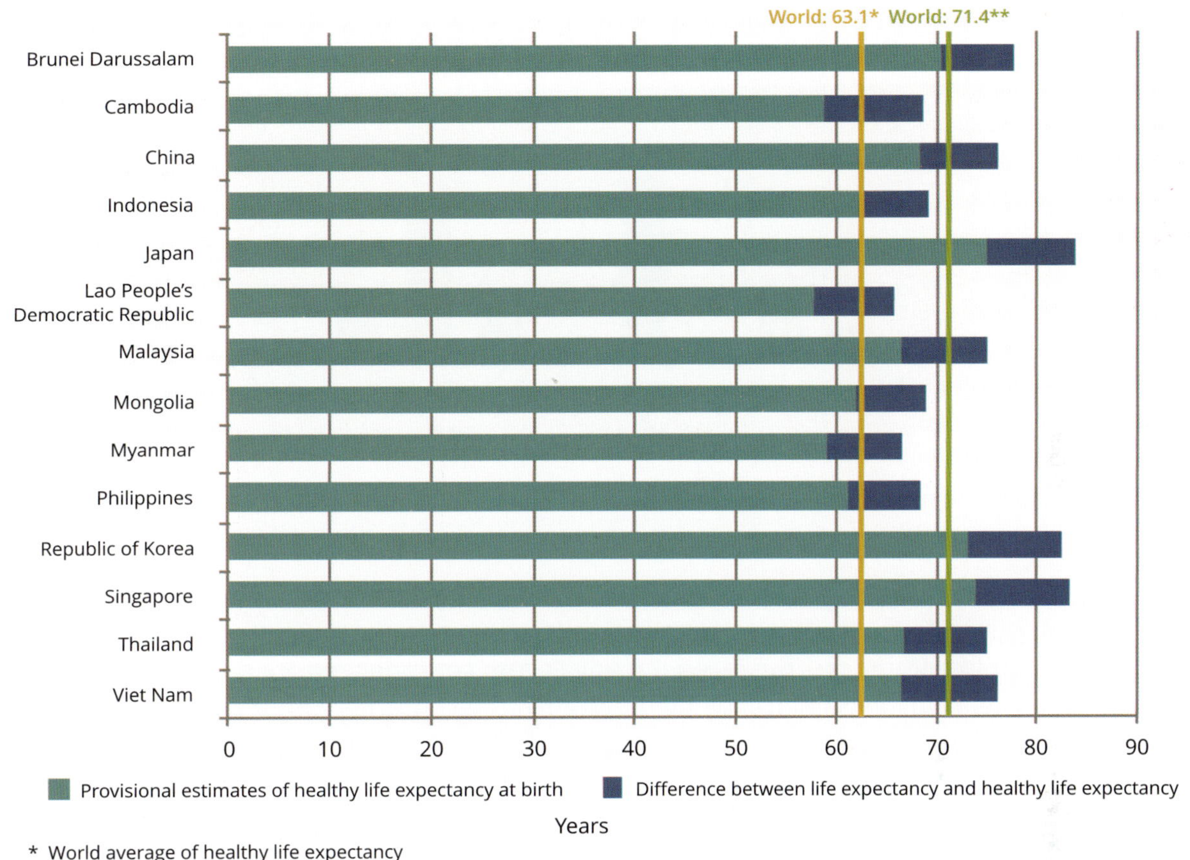

* World average of healthy life expectancy
** World average of life expectancy

Source: WHO, (2016d).

Fig. 16. Under-5 mortality rates per 1000 live births, 2015

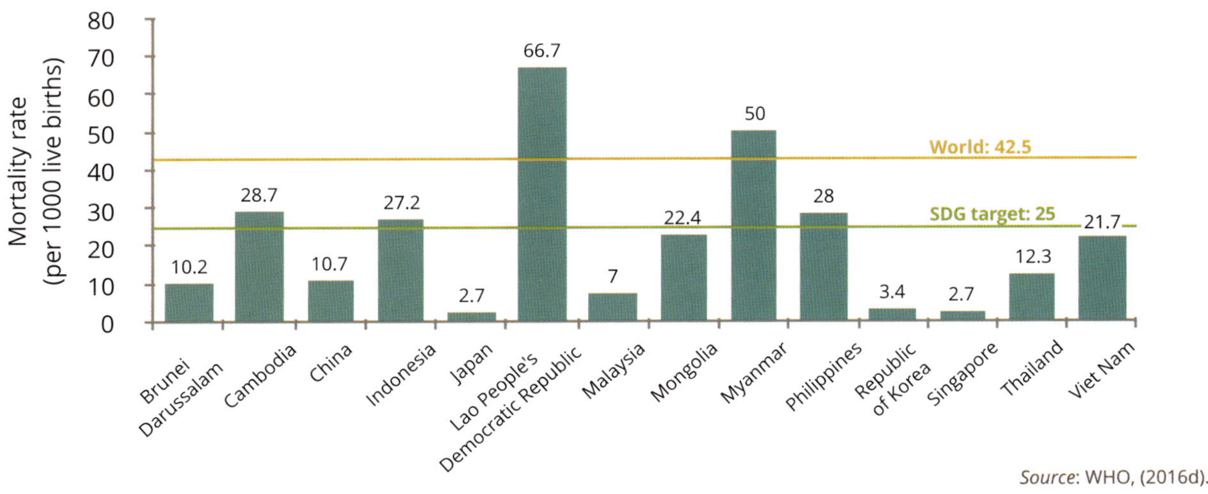

Source: WHO, (2016d).

Fig. 17. Neonatal mortality rates per 1000 live births, 2015

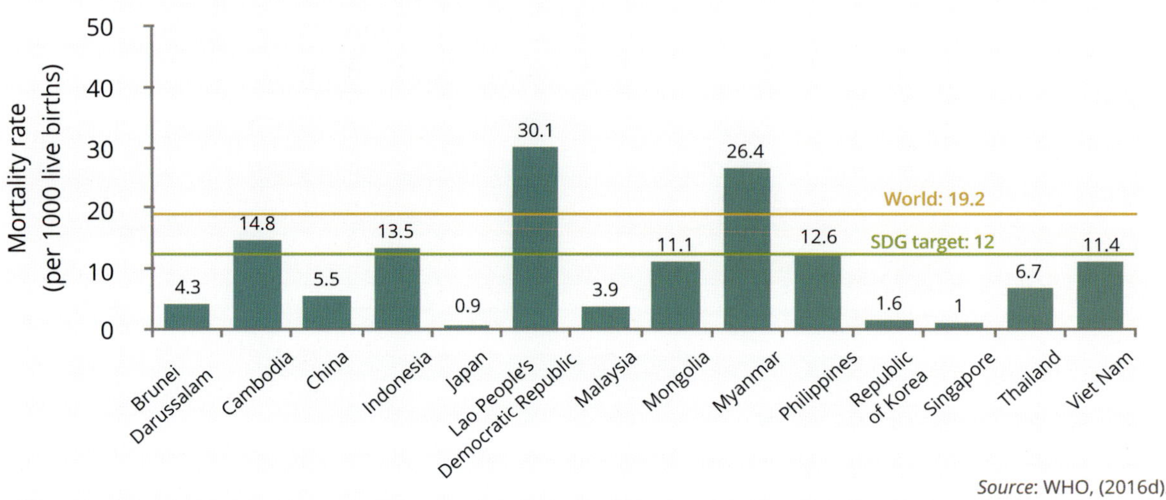

Source: WHO, (2016d).

SDG target 3.6 proposes to: by 2020, halve the number of global deaths and injuries from road traffic accidents. In Forum countries, death rates from road traffic range from 3.6 to 36 per 100 000, a 10-fold difference. Thus, even if many Forum countries reduce their mortality rates by half, they would still be significantly higher than in the countries with the lowest road traffic mortality. In 2013, only half of the Forum countries had mortality rates lower than the world average (Fig. 18).

Fig. 18. Road traffic mortality rate (per 100 000 population), 2013

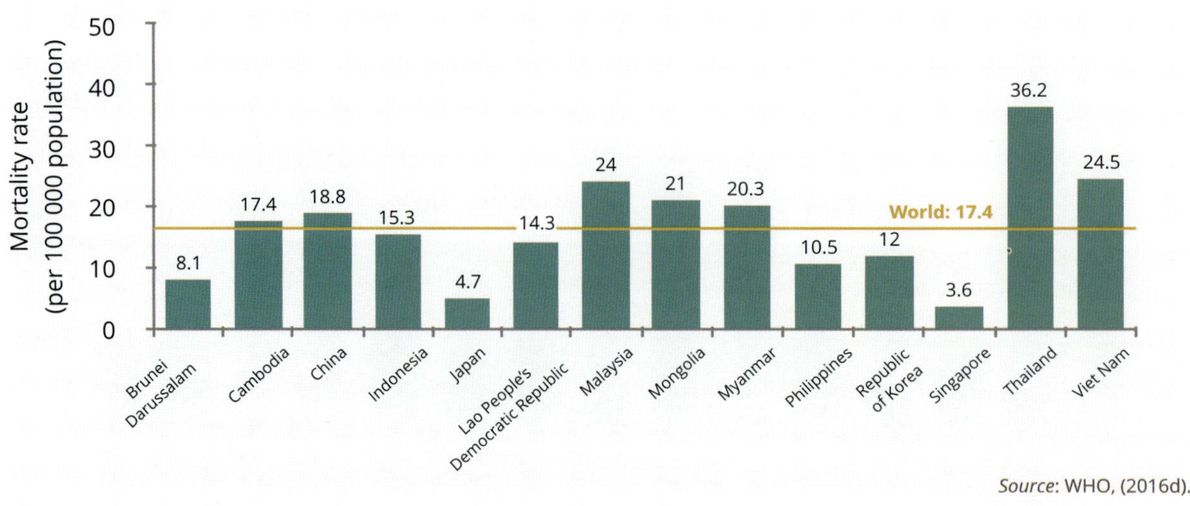

Source: WHO, (2016d).

In many Asian countries there are increased threats to health from widespread air pollution, chemicals and heavy metals (UNEP, 2016a). SDG target 3.9 proposes to: by 2030, substantially reduce the number of deaths and illnesses from hazardous chemicals and air, water and soil pollution and contamination. Fig. 19 shows mortality rates from combined household and ambient air pollution. Fig. 20 shows mortality rates from unintentional poisoning. There are large differences among the Forum countries. Air pollution mortality rates range from less than 1 to over 160 per 100 000.

Deaths from unintentional poisoning are lower, but significant. WHO maintains a database of poisons centres in countries. A poisons centre is a specialized unit that advises on, and assists with, the prevention, diagnosis and management of poisoning. The structure and function of poisons centres vary around the world; however, at a minimum a poisons centre is an information service. Some poisons centres may also include a toxicology laboratory and/or a clinical treatment unit. Poisons centres in WHO's database include 10 of the 14 Forum countries (WHO, 2016j).

Many countries produce and/or suffer from transboundary haze pollution. Member States of the Association of Southeast Asian Nations (ASEAN) signed the ASEAN Agreement on Transboundary Haze Pollution in 2002. The purpose of the agreement is to prevent, monitor as well as to strengthen mitigate land and forest fires to control transboundary haze pollution through concerted national efforts, and regional and international collaboration (ASEAN, 2002).

The Basel Convention on the Control of Transboundary Movements of Hazardous Wastes and their Disposal has the overarching objective of protecting human health and the environment against the adverse effects of hazardous waste. The Convention was adopted in March 1989, and the 14 Forum countries are Parties to the Convention (Basel Convention, 2016).

Fig. 19. Mortality rates from household and ambient air pollution, per 100 000, 2012

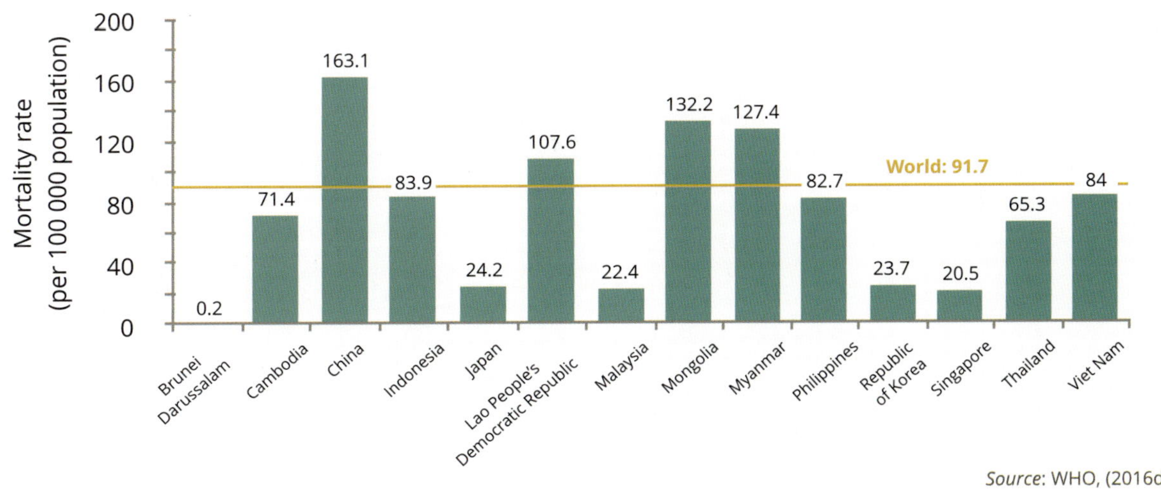

Source: WHO, (2016d).

Fig. 20. Mortality rates from unintentional poisoning, per 100 000 population, 2012

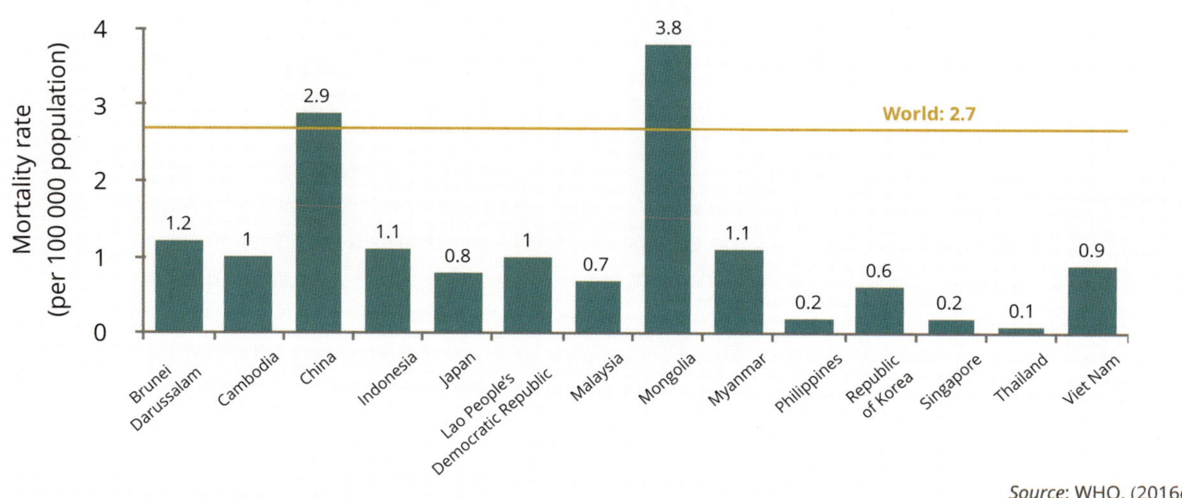

Source: WHO, (2016d).

National Environmental Health Action Plans

National Environmental Health Action Plans (NEHAPs) are a process of developing, adopting, implementing and evaluating environmental health policy. NEHAPs represent a comprehensive, holistic and intersectoral way of planning and implementing environmental health action at the national level. All Forum countries have produced NEHAPs.

Source: WHO/UNEP, (2005).

Brunei Darussalam: Top causes of death may have an environmental component

The top five causes of deaths in Brunei Darussalam (2012) were ischaemic heart disease (18.1%), stroke (11.2%), diabetes mellitus (10.7%), COPD (4.5%) and lower respiratory infections (4.1%). These five diseases contribute to nearly 50% of the burden of disease. At the global level, these diseases have a significant environmental component. For example, globally the environmental attributable fractions are 35% for ischaemic heart disease, 42% for stroke, 35% for COPD and 35% for lower respiratory infections.

Sources: WHO, (2015b) and WHO, (2016a).

EMERGING CHALLENGES

The rapid acceleration of human activity since the middle of the 20th century, characterized by rapid economic growth and a fast pace of production and consumption, is changing the planet. Destruction of ecosystems and a changing climate are altering weather patterns, exacerbating droughts and floods, affecting agriculture, water sources, disease vectors, and, in consequence, human health. These changes are proving difficult to control, even with several international agreements in place. The consequences for human health and well-being are keenly felt by vulnerable groups, including the urban and rural poor and those whose subsistence depends directly on the land, water or oceans. But the impacts include wealthy and poor countries alike. Global environmental changes, if not addressed with the urgency they deserve, have the potential to increase existing inequalities within and between countries. Fig. 21 shows annual water withdrawals in Forum countries, as a percentage of their total renewable water resources. Countries could be defined as water-stressed if they withdraw more than 25% of their renewable freshwater resources.

Climate change is the global change driver of greatest concern, because it is affecting other major global change issues, such as loss of biodiversity and desertification. All countries are similarly threatened by climate change, although the precise pathway, whether through increases in temperature (heatwaves), climate-related disasters, availability of water and food, or the spread of vectorborne diseases, may vary from place to place. Most importantly, what a country does to adapt and build resilience is key to avoiding, or at least reducing, health impacts.

Investing in a healthy environment is investing in the health and well-being of current and future generations.

UN Environment (2016b)

Fig. 21. Freshwater withdrawals (% of total renewable water resources per year), 2007–2011

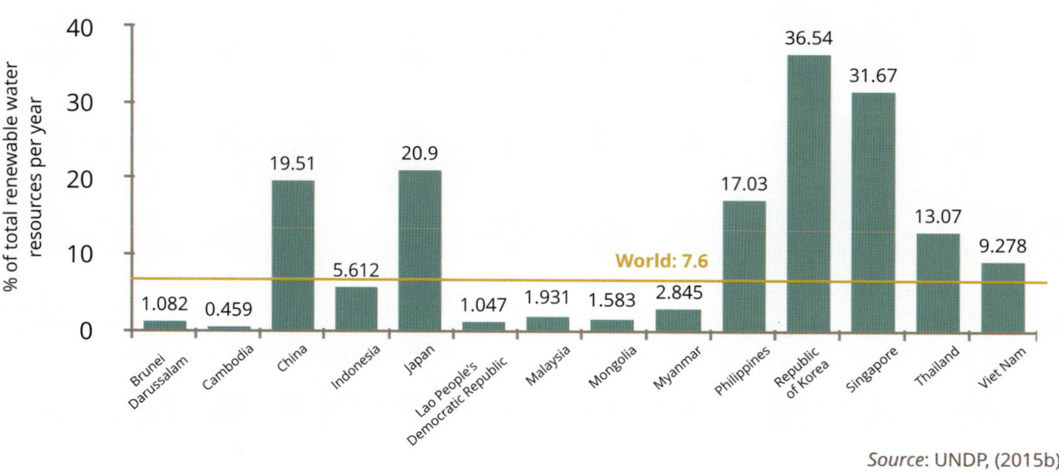

Source: UNDP, (2015b).

The United Nations Environment Programme (UNEP, 2016b) recommends four integrated lines of action to address current challenges.

- Detoxify, that is, to remove harmful substances from and/or mitigate their impact on the environment in which people live and work.
- Decarbonize, by reducing the use of carbon fuels and thereby emissions of CO_2 through substitution with renewable energy.
- Decouple resource use and change lifestyles – generate the needed economic activity and value to sustain the world's population with less resource use, less waste, less pollution and less environmental destruction.
- Enhance ecosystem resilience and protection of the planet's natural system, in recognition that only a healthy planet can sustain healthy life and healthy people.

Ecosystems and health

There is growing recognition of the importance of biodiversity, ecosystems and the services they provide as a foundation for sustainable development, human health and well-being. Loss of biodiversity and ecosystem disruption caused by human-induced factors, such as habitat destruction, over-exploitation, pollution and invasive alien species, affect the sustainability of production systems and lead to direct and indirect negative effects on human health, such as reduced food security and nutrition, increased water scarcity, increased flooding and infectious diseases, and loss of traditional medicines.

Source: UNEP ROAP, (2015).

Climate change, biological diversity and desertification threats in Mongolia

Mongolia is highly vulnerable to climate change due to its geographic location, fragile ecosystem and economy highly dependent on nature and weather conditions. The ecosystem of Mongolia has undergone considerable change in the past 40 years as a result of global climate change and human activity. This has manifested in growing desertification, increased frequency of drought and *dzud*, and decreased biological diversity and water resources. These manifestations of climate change have escalated to a point where they negatively affect human livelihoods.

Source: WHO, Environmental Health Country Report at the Regional Forum Meeting, 2016.

CONCLUSIONS

Working together in the spirit of leaving no one behind

Significant progress has been achieved in recent years but inequalities persist. All Forum countries have advanced in many aspects of environment and health. However, much remains to be done. Urban–rural differences, intra-urban differences and intercountry differences persist. Inequalities need to be addressed within and between Forum countries in recognition of the principle of solidarity of leaving no one behind. This spirit could transcend Forum countries and influence the work and behaviour of other countries and subregions, for the common benefit of our environment and our health.

Climate change adaptation and mitigation required urgently

Climate change makes our environment and health worse. Both reducing our impact on the environment to avoid further ecosystem disruptions and implementing adaptation measures for the change we cannot avoid are urgently required. Above all, efforts must focus on protecting the most vulnerable. Depending on the setting, this includes the rural and urban poor, agricultural workers, children, older people, pregnant women and self-sufficient communities.

All Sustainable Development Goals converge on health

The 17 SDGs and their 169 targets are interlinked. Many have in common the influence they have on human health and well-being. Although this synthesis focuses on those SDGs most likely to directly influence environment and health, there is no question about the importance of seeing all SDGs interacting and impacting on health and well-being. Addressing SDG linkages will protect and promote health.

Developing a core indicator set to monitor progress

Countries need information to monitor progress and to evaluate the performance of their interventions. Data overload, however, can be counterproductive and often a core set of valuable indicators is preferred. Forum countries have an opportunity to link this effort to SDG indicators to monitor performance and progress, with the support of the secretariats of WHO and UN Environment.

REFERENCES

ASEAN (2002). ASEAN agreement on transboundary haze pollution (http://environment.asean.org/wp-content/uploads/2015/06/ASEANAgreementonTransboundaryHazePollution.pdf).

ASEAN/UNICEF/WHO (2016). Regional report on nutrition security in ASEAN Vol 2. Bangkok: UNICEF (http://www.searo.who.int/entity/nutrition/regional_report_on_nutrition_security_in_asean_volume_2.pdf?ua=1).

Basel Convention (2016). Status of Ratification (http://www.basel.int/Countries/StatusofRatifications/PartiesSignatories/tabid/4499/Default.aspx).

Centre for Research on the Epidemiology of Disasters (CRED, 2016) (http://www.emdat.be/).

Lao People's Democratic Republic (2015). Intended Nationally Determined Contribution (http://www4.unfccc.int/Submissions/INDC/Published%20Documents/Laos/1/Lao%20PDR%20INDC.pdf).

UNDP (2015a). Human Development Data (1980–2015) (http://hdr.undp.org/en/data#).

UNDP (2015b). World Development Report 2015: Work for human development (http://hr.undp.org/sites/default/files/2015_human_development_report.pdf).

UN Environment ROAP (2015). First Forum of Ministers and Environment Authorities of Asia Pacific, Bangkok, 19–20 May 2015 (http://www.unep.org/geo/assessments/regional-assessments/regional-assessment-asia-and-pacific).

UN Environment (2016a). GEO-6 Regional assessment for Asia and the Pacific (http://www.unep.org/geo/assessments/regional-assessments/regional-assessment-asia-and-pacific).

UN Environment (2016b). Healthy Environment, Healthy People. Thematic report: Ministerial policy review session: Second session of the United Nations Environment Assembly of the United Nations Environment Programme. Nairobi, 23–27 May 2016 (http://www.unep.org/about/sgb/Portals/ 50153/UNEA/K1602727%20INF%205.pdf).

United Nations (2012). Resolution adopted by the General Assembly on 27 July 2012. 66/288, The Future We Want (http://www.un.org/ga/search/view_doc.asp?symbol=ARES/66/288&Lang=E).

United Nations (2014). World Urbanization Prospects 2014 revision (https://esa.un.org/unpd/wup/CD-ROM/).

United Nations (2015a). Resolution adopted by the General Assembly on 25 September 2015. Transforming our world: the 2030 Agenda for Sustainable Development (http://www.un.org/ga/search/view_doc.asp?symbol=A/RES/70/1&Lang=E).

United Nations (2015b). Millennium Development Goals Indicators. Slum population in urban areas (http://mdgs.un.org/unsd/mdg/SeriesDetail.aspx?srid=711).

WHO (2013). Global Health Observatory data repository. Population using solid fuels (estimates) (http://apps.who.int/gho/data/view.main.1681?lang=en).

WHO (2014). Global Health Observatory data repository. Ambient air pollution burden of disease (http://apps.who.int/gho/data/node.main.156?lang=en).

WHO (2015a). Climate change and health in the Western Pacific Region.

WHO (2015b). Country statistics (http://www.who.int/gho/countries/brn.pdf?ua=1).

WHO (2015c). Drinking water (http://www.who.int/mediacentre/factsheets/fs391/en/).

WHO (2015d). Food safety (http://www.who.int/mediacentre/factsheets/fs399/en/).

WHO (2016a). Preventing disease through healthy environments: a global assessment of the burden of disease from environmental risks (http://apps.who.int/iris/bitstream/10665/204585/1/9789241565196_eng.pdf?ua=1).

WHO (2016b). Preventing disease through healthy environments: a global assessment of the burden of disease from environmental risks. Global Health Observatory Data (http://www.who.int/entity/quantifying_ehimpacts/publications/Age-stand_by_country_GHO_final.xls?ua=1).

WHO (2016c). Children: reducing mortality (http://www.who.int/mediacentre/factsheets/fs178/en/).

WHO (2016d). World Health Statistics 2016 – Monitoring health for the SDGs (http://apps.who.int/iris/bitstream/10665/206498/1/9789241565264_eng.pdf).

WHO (2016e). Household air pollution and health (http://www.who.int/mediacentre/factsheets/fs292/en/).

WHO (2016f). Ambient air pollution: a global assessment of exposure and burden of disease (http://apps.who.int/iris/bitstream/10665/250141/1/9789241511353-eng.pdf).

WHO (2016g). Air pollution database 2016 (http://www.who.int/entity/phe/health_topics/outdoorair/databases/WHO_AAP_database_May2016_v3web.xlsx?ua=1).

WHO (2016h). Climate change and health (http://www.who.int/mediacentre/factsheets/fs266/en/).

WHO (2016i). The Paris agreement (http://www.who.int/globalchange/mediacentre/events/climate-health-conference/en/).

WHO (2016j). World directory of poisons centres (http://www.who.int/gho/phe/chemical_safety/poisons_centres/en/).

WHO/UNEP (2005). National Environmental Health Action Plans (NEHAPs) (http://www.who.int/heli/impacts/nehaps/en/).

WHO/UNICEF (2015a). Joint Monitoring Programme (JMP) for water supply and sanitation. Data and estimates (http://www.wssinfo.org/data-estimates/).

WHO/UNICEF (2015b). Joint Monitoring Programme (JMP) for water supply and sanitation. Progress on sanitation and drinking water. 2015 update and MDG assessment (http://www.wssinfo.org/fileadmin/user_upload/resources/JMP-Update-report-2015_English.pdf).